COM PLA CEN CY

LUKE 2:52

Ministry is not a place to settle... It's a place to stir up the gift. If things feel stuck, God is still speaking. These next steps are to help you listen again, move again, and lead with fresh oil.

THE LAND OF COPE

A Pastoral Leadership Guide to Accountability for Pastors

Rev. Leonard Huggins, Jr.

Cover by: Sharon Lewis-Ruff, The Planner Consulting
Editing by: Sharon Lewis-Ruff
Formatting by: Wisdom by 30 Literary Group

ISBN: 979-8-9942619-1-0
ISBN Digital: 979-8-9942619-1-0

What am I avoiding in this season—emotionally, spiritually, or relationally—that may be keeping me in a place of comfort instead of calling?

_____

_____

_____

_____

What do I say "yes" to that secretly drains me, and what do I avoid that I know would grow me?

_____

_____

_____

_____

What patterns, routines, or comforts have slowly replaced my hunger for God's voice and presence?

_____

_____

_____

_____

Where have I settled for "good enough" when God has called me to growth?

Am I maintaining a version of ministry/business that looks successful on the outside but feels empty behind the scenes?

What's one area in my life or leadership that God has whispered about, but I keep putting off?

REFLECTIONS

_____

_____

_____

_____

_____

_____

_____

_____

_____

_____

_____

NOTES FOR FUTURE SERMON(S)

REFLECTIONS

_____

_____

_____

_____

_____

_____

_____

_____

_____

_____

_____

NOTES FOR FUTURE SERMON(S)

CON
STR
UCT

You were never meant to carry the vision alone.

Jesus had a team. So should you. These pages are here to help you build wisely, delegate well, and grow together.

What kind of a team do you need?

_____

_____

_____

_____

What are the core values my team must carry—not just skills, but spirit, character, and culture?

_____

_____

_____

_____

Am I seeking people who can execute my vision—or am I open to people who will challenge and expand it? How?

_____

_____

_____

_____

What gaps exist on my current team (or in my current mindset) that are keeping us from being spiritually sharp and strategically sound?

_____

_____

_____

_____

Am I willing to release people when their season is up—or do I struggle with loyalty over leadership clarity?

_____

_____

_____

_____

What do I tend to hold onto too tightly because of control, fear, or pride—and how is that limiting my team's growth?

_____

_____

_____

_____

ACTION PAGE

Who is missing from your current team dynamic?

_____

_____

Are you over-relying on any one person or type? What's the risk of that?

_____

_____

What steps do you need to take to pray for, prepare for, or pursue the team you actually need?

_____

_____

What internal work do you need to do to delegate with trust and lead without micromanaging?

_____

_____

Action Plan (Next 30 Days)

Recruit _____

Release _____

Realign _____

TEAM ROLES

Team Member's Name	Primary Role	Spiritual Alignment (1-5)	Skill Alignment (1-5)	Trust Level 1-5	Notes/ Concerns

BUILD A TEAM

REFLECTIONS

_____

_____

_____

_____

_____

_____

_____

_____

_____

_____

_____

_____

NOTES FOR FUTURE SERMON(S)

REFLECTIONS

_____

_____

_____

_____

_____

_____

_____

_____

_____

_____

_____

_____

NOTES FOR FUTURE SERMON(S)

OR DER

God is not the author of confusion, and neither should we allow it in His house.

This section will equip you with prayerful and pastoral approaches to guard the peace of your ministry with grace and authority.

Have I created a culture where honest correction is embraced—or where silence is misused as spiritual maturity?

_____

_____

_____

_____

Am I trying to rehabilitate what God is revealing as rebellion?

_____

_____

_____

_____

Have I clearly communicated expectations, boundaries, and the vision—or have I left space for personal agendas to take root?

_____

_____

_____

_____

What's the root of the discord—jealousy, offense, pride, misunderstanding, fear of being replaced?

Who am I protecting by not addressing this?

How do I model grace and truth in correction—without enabling spiritual manipulation or emotional immaturity?

Pray + journal: God, what is the root? What is my response supposed to be—confront, correct, cover, or release?

_____

_____

_____

_____

_____

_____

_____

_____

_____

Write a truth-centered affirmation to remind yourself:

_____

_____

_____

_____

NEGATIVITY

REFLECTIONS

_____

_____

_____

_____

_____

_____

_____

_____

_____

_____

_____

NOTES FOR FUTURE SERMON(S)

REFLECTIONS

_____

_____

_____

_____

_____

_____

_____

_____

_____

_____

_____

_____

NOTES FOR FUTURE SERMON(S)

MEM BER SHIP

ROMANS 16:17

Don't count heads, build hearts.

What looks small in the natural can still make a great impact on the Spirit. Let this be your season to rebuild by faith, not by sight.

CLARITY PAGE

What is the mission of your church in one sentence?

_____

_____

Does your current ministry activity reflect that mission?

☐ *Yes*
☐ *No*

If no, what needs to change?

_____

_____

List 3 faith-centered goals for your ministry in the next 6 months:

_____

_____

_____

_____

_____

Check all that apply to your current congregation:

☐ *Members feel spiritually fed*
☐ *Members want to grow, but lack direction*
☐ *Members want to serve but need guidance*
☐ *Members are tired or burned out*
☐ *Members are unaware of their gifts*

List 3 active members. What are their strengths or spiritual gifts?

NAME	STRENGTH/ SPIRITUAL GIFT	WAY TO USE IT IN MINISTRY

Write a short affirmation for your congregation that shifts focus from numbers to faith-building: **"Our church may be small in number, but we are rich in faith because..."**

───

───

───

───

What is one way you can strengthen discipleship in your church right now?

───

───

───

───

What is one area where your members can be encouraged to trust God more deeply? (Check all that apply)

□ *Finances*   □ *Leadership*
□ *Health*   □ *Evangelism*
□ *Forgiveness*

□ *Other:*

─────────────────────────────

What does "building faith" mean in your current context of ministry?

_____

_____

_____

_____

In what ways can small membership be a spiritual advantage?

_____

_____

_____

_____

How have you personally measured "success" in ministry?
(Check all that apply)

☐ Membership size   ☐ Consistent attendance
☐ Tithes/Offerings   ☐ Community impact
☐ Spiritual growth of members   ☐ Testimonies/transformations

☐ Other:

_____

How can a clear, written vision help your small congregation stay focused?

Write 1 creative way you can encourage participation from those who are less involved:

In what ways are you modeling trust in God to your congregation?

What is one area of ministry where you've been tempted to rely more on strategy than faith?

_____

_____

_____

_____

Use this guide to write your own weekly faith confession for your leadership team:
"We declare that God is faithful. Though we are small in number, we are mighty in Spirit. This week, we trust God to..."

_____

_____

_____

_____

_____

_____

_____

_____

REFLECTIONS

_____

_____

_____

_____

_____

_____

_____

_____

_____

_____

_____

NOTES FOR FUTURE SERMON(S)

REFLECTIONS

_____

_____

_____

_____

_____

_____

_____

_____

_____

_____

_____

NOTES FOR FUTURE SERMON(S)

PAR SON AGE

ROMANS 16:17

Your home should be a place of peace, not pressure. Whether you live in a parsonage or your own home, this section is meant to help you protect your family and honor the space God has given you.

How can a strong home life strengthen your public ministry?

_____

_____

_____

Activity	Hours Spent	Fulfills Family?	Fulfills Ministry?	Should Adjust?
Counseling/Meetings				
Date Night				
Family Time				
Phone Calls/Emails				
Self-Care (rest, prayer)				

How do we support each other's calling?

_____

_____

_____

_____

Are we allowing ministry to take the place of our marriage?
If yes or sometimes, what boundaries need to be set?

☐ *Yes*
☐ *Sometimes*
☐ *No*

One thing I love and appreciate about my spouse in ministry:

_____

_____

_____

Rate the following areas on a scale of 1–5 (1 = Needs work, 5 = Very strong)

Area	Rating
Communication	
Conflict Resolution	
Intimacy (Emotional & Physical)	
Ministry Alignment	
Quality Time Together	

How do we support each other's calling?

Commit to a 30-minute weekly check-in using these 3 prompts:

- What was the best part of our week together?
- How can I support you better this week?
- How are we spiritually?

Record a few thoughts after your first check-in here:

_____

_____

_____

_____

How do your children feel about the ministry you serve in?

☐ They love it
☐ They feel left out
☐ They don't understand it
☐ They are frustrated with it

Describe what they've said or shown:

_____

_____

How can you include your children in ministry without overwhelming them?

_____

_____

_____

_____

Check the ones you want to prioritize:

☐ I will protect family time like I protect church time
☐ I will speak positively about the church around my kids
☐ I will listen to their frustrations without judgment
☐ I will not compare them to "perfect church kids"
☐ I will help them discover their own relationship with God

"Father, help me to raise children who know You personally, not just through my role. Give me wisdom to guide them, patience to nurture them, and grace to cover them as I serve You."

Write your own prayer for your children below:

_____

_____

_____

_____

REFLECTIONS

_____

_____

_____

_____

_____

_____

_____

_____

_____

_____

_____

NOTES FOR FUTURE SERMON(S)

REFLECTIONS

NOTES FOR FUTURE SERMON(S)

ACC OUNT A BILITY

ROMANS 16:17

When done with the right heart, evaluation becomes a tool for spiritual growth, not just for the leader, but for the entire congregation. It helps the pastor grow deeper in the Lord, remain accountable in their calling, and stay aligned with the needs of the people they serve.

Evaluation is not about criticism; it's about clarity, connection, and confirming that we are walking in step with the vision God has given us. It also allows us to ask important questions together:

Are we growing in faith?
Are lives being transformed?
Are we reaching the goals God set before us?

2 TIMOTHY 1:7

PASTOR EVALUATION

YES, PASTORS SHOULD BE LOVINGLY AND PRAYERFULLY EVALUATED.

		POOR	GOOD
01	HOW MANY CONFESS JESUS AS THEIR LORD SAVIOR THIS YEAR?	☐	☐
02	INCREASE IN SUNDAY SCHOOL OR BIBLE STUDY ATTENDANCE IN THE LAST SIX MONTHS?	☐	☐
03	INCREASE IN TITHES AND OFFERINGS IN THE LAST THREE MONTHS?	☐	☐
04	IS THE PASTOR DEVELOPING NEW LEADERS?	☐	☐
05	IS THE PAST AWARE OF THE NEEDS OF THE CONGREGATION?	☐	☐
06	DO THE SERMONS HAVE CLEAR BIBLICAL INSTRUCTION?	☐	☐
07	THE PASTOR IS GOOD AT RESOLVING CONFLICT IN THE CHURCH.	☐	☐
08	IS THE PASTOR A GOOD LISTENER?	☐	☐

PASTOR EVALUATION

YES, PASTORS SHOULD BE LOVINGLY AND PRAYERFULLY EVALUATED.

09	DOES THE PASTOR ACCEPT ACCOUNTABILITY WELL?	POOR ☐	GOOD ☐
10	DOES THE PASTOR ENCOURAGE MEMBERS TO INVITE OTHERS TO THE WORSHIP SERVICES?	POOR ☐	GOOD ☐
11	DOES THE PASTOR PREACH OR TEACH ON EVANGELISM REGULARLY?	POOR ☐	GOOD ☐

REFLECTIONS

NOTES FOR FUTURE SERMON(S)

REFLECTIONS

_____

_____

_____

_____

_____

_____

_____

_____

_____

_____

_____

NOTES FOR FUTURE SERMON(S)

VI SION

ROMANS 16:17

Where there is no vision, the people perish.

But where there is God's vision, there is purpose, provision, and progress. Use these pages to get clear and then move forward boldly.

VISION PLANNING

Theme for the Year
What is the central spiritual theme God is placing on your heart for the year?

_____

_____

Spiritual Focus
Scriptures that will anchor this year's preaching and teaching:

_____

_____

Spiritual Focus
Personal spiritual disciplines I will strengthen this year:

_____

_____

Congregational Health
Greatest spiritual needs in the congregation right now:

_____

_____

VISION PLANNING

Congregational Health
Ways to equip the congregation for spiritual maturity:

_____

_____

Outreach & Community Impact
Community outreach initiatives for the year:

_____

_____

Outreach & Community Impact
Potential ministry partners or collaborators:

_____

_____

Leadership Development
Leaders or emerging leaders who need mentoring:

_____

_____

VISION PLANNING

Family & Self-Care Balance
Plans to guard rest, family, and personal growth:

_____

_____

Family & Self-Care Balance
Boundaries that need to be communicated and upheld:

_____

_____

Reflection for Year 1:
What do I believe God wants to establish this year that will outlast me?

_____

_____

_____

_____

VISION PLANNING

Evaluating Impact
- How will we measure spiritual progress?
- Salvations
- Baptisms
- Attendance Growth
- Testimonies
- Community Reach
- Other:

_____

_____

_____

_____

_____

_____

_____

_____

_____

_____

REFLECTIONS

_____

_____

_____

_____

_____

_____

_____

_____

_____

_____

_____

NOTES FOR FUTURE SERMON(S)

REFLECTIONS

NOTES FOR FUTURE SERMON(S)

EX
ITS

Loss doesn't mean failure. It means it's time to learn, listen, and lead differently.

This section will guide you in leaving the door open for grace, growth, and reconciliation when members leave the church.

MEMBER REFLECTIONS

What initially drew you to our church?

_____

_____

How long have you been part of the ministry?

_____

_____

What aspects of your experience here were most meaningful?

☐ *Worship*
☐ *Teaching/Preaching*
☐ *Fellowship/Community*
☐ *Outreach/Ministry Opportunities*
☐ *Other:* _____

_____

_____

_____

_____

MEMBER REFLECTIONS

Are there areas where you felt disconnected or unfulfilled?

_____

_____

What led to your decision to leave at this time?

☐ *Relocating*
☐ *Seeking a different worship style or denomination*
☐ *Interpersonal conflict*
☐ *Family decision*
☐ *Spiritual leadership*
☐ *Other:* _____

_____

_____

_____

_____

Do you feel your concerns or needs were heard while you were here?

☐ *Yes*
☐ *No*
☐ *Somewhat*

MEMBER REFLECTIONS

Would you like continued pastoral care during your transition?

☐ *Yes*
☐ *No*
☐ *Maybe, depending on circumstances*

What could we as a church have done better to support you or your family?

_____

_____

_____

_____

What could we as a church have done better to support you or your family?

_____

_____

_____

_____

Are you open to returning in the future if led by the Spirit or circumstances change?

☐ *Yes*
☐ *No*
☐ *Somewhat*

Thank you for your time, service, and presence.
No matter where God leads you next, we pray for
His favor, peace, and purpose to follow you. You
are always loved here.

ROMAN 15:13

NO
TES

REFLECTIONS

_____

_____

_____

_____

_____

_____

_____

_____

_____

_____

_____

NOTES FOR FUTURE SERMON(S)

REFLECTIONS

_____

_____

_____

_____

_____

_____

_____

_____

_____

_____

_____

NOTES FOR FUTURE SERMON(S)

REFLECTIONS

_____

_____

_____

_____

_____

_____

_____

_____

_____

_____

_____

NOTES FOR FUTURE SERMON(S)

REFLECTIONS

_____

_____

_____

_____

_____

_____

_____

_____

_____

_____

_____

_____

NOTES FOR FUTURE SERMON(S)

REFLECTIONS

_____

_____

_____

_____

_____

_____

_____

_____

_____

_____

_____

NOTES FOR FUTURE SERMON(S)

REFLECTIONS

_____

_____

_____

_____

_____

_____

_____

_____

_____

_____

_____

NOTES FOR FUTURE SERMON(S)

REFLECTIONS

NOTES FOR FUTURE SERMON(S)

REFLECTIONS

_____

_____

_____

_____

_____

_____

_____

_____

_____

_____

_____

NOTES FOR FUTURE SERMON(S)

REFLECTIONS

_____

_____

_____

_____

_____

_____

_____

_____

_____

_____

_____

NOTES FOR FUTURE SERMON(S)

REFLECTIONS

_____

_____

_____

_____

_____

_____

_____

_____

_____

_____

_____

NOTES FOR FUTURE SERMON(S)

REFLECTIONS

_____

_____

_____

_____

_____

_____

_____

_____

_____

_____

_____

NOTES FOR FUTURE SERMON(S)

REFLECTIONS

_____

_____

_____

_____

_____

_____

_____

_____

_____

_____

_____

_____

NOTES FOR FUTURE SERMON(S)

REFLECTIONS

_____

_____

_____

_____

_____

_____

_____

_____

_____

_____

_____

NOTES FOR FUTURE SERMON(S)

REFLECTIONS

_____

_____

_____

_____

_____

_____

_____

_____

_____

_____

_____

NOTES FOR FUTURE SERMON(S)

REFLECTIONS

_____

_____

_____

_____

_____

_____

_____

_____

_____

_____

_____

NOTES FOR FUTURE SERMON(S)

Father, we thank You for the shepherds You've entrusted with Your people.

As they have labored over these pages with honesty and hope, we ask that You breathe fresh life into every dream, every vision, and every challenge.

Rekindle their fire, renew their strength, and restore anything that has been lost. Give them eyes to see, ears to hear, and hearts that discern the move of Your Spirit.

Cover their families, unify their teams, and build up their congregations in faith and love. Let their leadership be marked by grace, wisdom, and compassion. In all things, may Your name be glorified. In Jesus' name, amen.

Rev. Leonard Huggins, Jr.